mm

Spotlight on
Egypt

Bobbie Kalman

Crabtree Publishing Company

www.crabtreebooks.com

Spotlight On My Country

Created by Bobbie Kalman

Dedicated by Emese Felvégi
For my family

Editor-in-Chief
Bobbie Kalman

Writing team
Bobbie Kalman
Emese Felvégi

Editor
Kathy Middleton

Proofreader
Crystal Sikkens

Fact editor
Marcella Haanstra

Photo research
Bobbie Kalman
Emese Felvégi

Design
Bobbie Kalman
Katherine Berti

Print and production coordinator
Katherine Berti

Prepress technician
Katherine Berti

Illustrations
Katherine Berti: pages 4, 5 (top)

Photographs
BigStockPhoto: page 10 (inset left)
Peter and Marc Crabtree: pages 6,
    12 (top and bottom), 13, 22 (bottom),
    31 (bottom)
Photos.com: pages 24, 29 (dates),
    31 (top left)
Cover and all other images by Shutterstock

Library and Archives Canada Cataloguing in Publication

Kalman, Bobbie, 1947-
    Spotlight on Egypt / Bobbie Kalman.

(Spotlight on my country)
Includes index.
Issued also in an electronic format.
ISBN 978-0-7787-3457-4 (bound).--ISBN 978-0-7787-3483-3 (pbk.)

    1. Egypt--Juvenile literature. I. Title. II. Series: Spotlight on
my country

DT49.K34 2011   j962   C2010-904122-4

Library of Congress Cataloging-in-Publication Data

Kalman, Bobbie.
 Spotlight on Egypt / Bobbie Kalman.
    p. cm. -- (Spotlight on my country)
 Includes index.
 ISBN 978-0-7787-3483-3 (pbk. : alk. paper) -- ISBN 978-0-7787-3457-4
(reinforced library binding : alk. paper) -- ISBN 978-1-4271-9536-4
(electronic (pdf))
 1. Egypt--Juvenile literature. 2. Egypt--Civilization--To 332 B.C.--
Juvenile literature. I. Title. II. Series.

 DT49.K35 2011
 962--dc22
                                                    2010024603

Crabtree Publishing Company

www.crabtreebooks.com   1-800-387-7650

Printed in the U.S.A./082010/BA20100709

Published in Canada
Crabtree Publishing
616 Welland Ave.
St. Catharines, Ontario
L2M 5V6

Published in the United States
Crabtree Publishing
PMB 59051
350 Fifth Avenue, 59th Floor
New York, New York 10118

Published in the United Kingdom
Crabtree Publishing
Maritime House
Basin Road North, Hove
BN41 1WR

Published in Australia
Crabtree Publishing
386 Mt. Alexander Rd.
Ascot Vale (Melbourne)
VIC 3032

Contents

Welcome to Egypt!

Egypt is a large **country**. A country is an area of land on which people live. Countries have **borders**, or imaginary lines that separate them from other countries. Egypt shares its borders with Libya, Sudan, the Gaza Strip, and Israel. Cairo is Egypt's capital city.

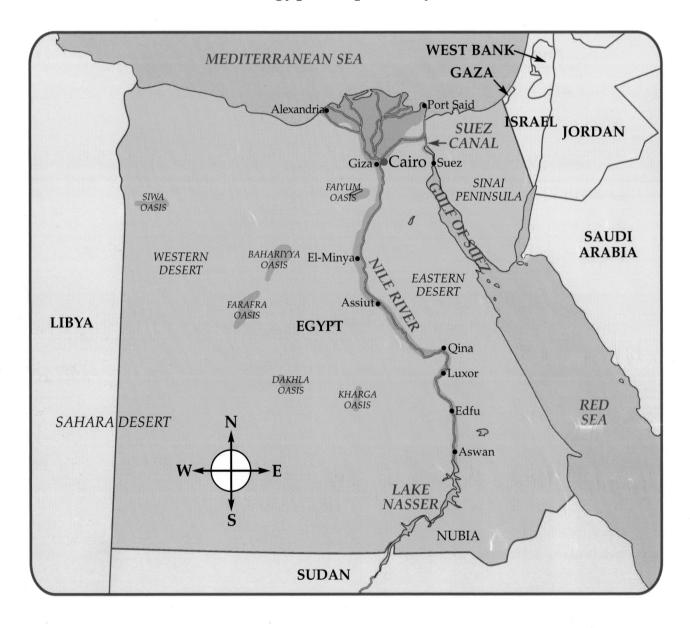

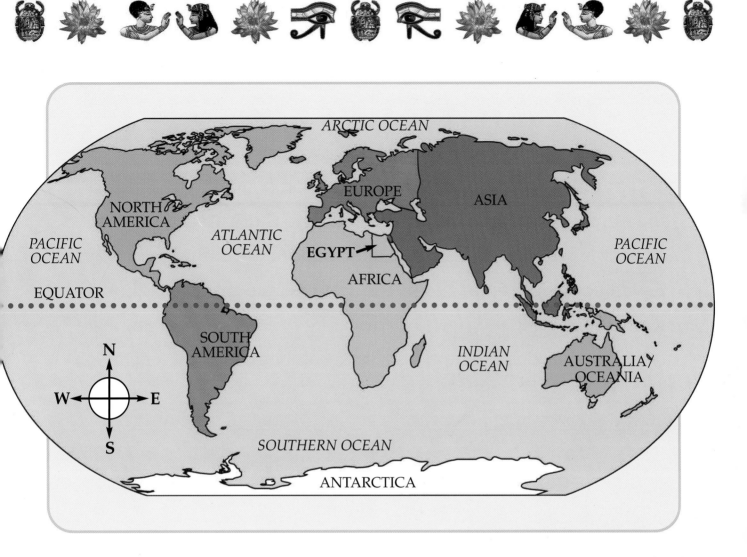

ARCTIC OCEAN

EUROPE

ASIA

NORTH
AMERICA

ATLANTIC
OCEAN

PACIFIC
OCEAN

EGYPT→

PACIFIC
OCEAN

AFRICA

EQUATOR

SOUTH
AMERICA

N

INDIAN
OCEAN

AUSTRALIA/
OCEANIA

W——E

S

SOUTHERN OCEAN

ANTARCTICA

Where in the world is Egypt?
Egypt is located in the **continent**
of Africa. A small part of Egypt
is in the continent of Asia.
A continent is a huge area of
land. The other continents are
North America, South America,
Europe, Australia/Oceania, and
Antarctica. The seven continents
are shown on the world map
above. Find Egypt on this map.

The people of Egypt

The **population** of Egypt is over 80 million people. Population is the number of people living in a country. There are four groups of people who live in Egypt: Arabs, Bedouins, Nubians, and the Siwan people. People who live in Egypt came from Asia, Europe, the Middle East, and parts of Africa. Egyptians speak a language called Arabic. Some Egyptians also speak English and French.

These schoolgirls come from different backgrounds, but they are all Egyptians.

Bedouins are traditionally **nomads**. Nomads live in one place for a short time and then move to another place. Some Bedouins still travel the **desert** by camel and raise sheep and goats to sell at markets. Today, however, most Bedouins have moved to the cities, where the men have jobs other than herding animals.

These girls are Nubians. Nubians have lived in southern Egypt for thousands of years.

Egyptians are a mix of many peoples, but most people who live in Egypt are Arabs.

The land of Egypt

Egypt's land areas are very different. The Nile River runs through the huge deserts of Egypt. The Western Desert takes up two thirds of Egypt's land area. The Eastern Desert lies between the Nile River and the Red Sea. Along the Nile River are farmlands. The Sinai **Peninsula**, which connects Africa to Asia, has some high mountains. A peninsula is land that is almost completely surrounded by water.

The Eastern Desert ends at the Red Sea. This area has a lot of oil.

*Many kinds of fish and other ocean animals live in the colorful **coral reefs** of the Red Sea. A coral reef is an underwater **habitat**, or natural home. Coral reefs are found in warm, shallow oceans and seas.*

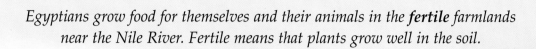

Egyptians grow food for themselves and their animals in the **fertile** farmlands near the Nile River. Fertile means that plants grow well in the soil.

Deserts are dry areas that get very little rain. Strong winds blow in deserts. The Western Desert has huge sand **dunes**. Dunes form when piles of sand are pushed around by the wind. The best way to travel on sand dunes is by camel.

sand dunes

The Nile River

The Nile is the longest river in the world. It is 4,132 miles (6,650 km) long. The river is very important to Egyptians because it provides water in a very dry country. The Nile River also provides food. People use the water from the river to grow **crops**, or plants that are grown as food. About three-quarters of Egypt's people live by the Nile River. They live in villages, small towns, and large cities, such as Cairo.

Feluccas are sailboats that have sailed on the Nile for thousands of years. This felucca captain takes tourists on sailboat rides.

The Nile River is a source of water, food, and transportation for Egyptians. These people are catching fish in the river to sell in the markets.

Cairo is on the Nile. Twenty million people live in this busy city and in the areas around it.

Nubia is a region along the Nile River in the south of Egypt. Most of Nubia is in Sudan, but about one-quarter is in Egypt. Nubian villages can be found on the west bank of the Nile. This colorful Nubian home is being visited by tourists who came by boat to see it.

felucca →

Life in Cairo

Most Egyptians today live in cities. Egyptian cities are a blend of old and new ways. These photographs show life in Cairo, Egypt's capital. People call Cairo "Mother of the World."

1. This Egyptian family is sightseeing and learning about the history of Egypt.

2. These Egyptian girls are looking at Cairo from a bridge above the city.

3. The streets of Cairo are crowded with people. This street is lined with shops.

4. Four teenage friends are meeting by the Nile River for a snack and a chat.

5. These children are helping their father sell vegetables from a cart at the side of a city street.

6. These young girls attend a **private school** in Cairo. They are learning English.

7. People meet at outdoor restaurants to talk and eat with their friends.

Desert life

The Sahara Desert covers most of Northern Africa. The desert receives only a few inches of rain each year. Today, most Egyptians travel across the desert by car. Some still travel by camel in groups called **caravans**. Caravans often ride for days without seeing plants or water.

*At the edge of the desert, farmers need to **irrigate**, or bring water to the crops in channels, such as the one shown above.*

*During the day, it is very hot in the desert. When heat reflects the sky over sand, we see a **mirage**. A mirage can look like a sheet of water on the sand.*

14

What is an oasis?

An oasis is a place in a desert where there is water under the ground. The underground water comes up to the surface naturally or through wells. Farms, villages, or even cities are built around large oases. The tall palms that grow in oases provide shade for people and for smaller plants. Caravans can find water and shelter in desert oases. Find the oases on the map on page 4.

keffiyeh

blanket

Bedouins wear loose clothing to protect them from hot and cold temperatures. Men wind keffiyehs, *or cotton cloths, around their heads and carry heavy blankets to shield them from sand storms and keep them warm at night. Women wear long, loose robes.*

Plants and animals

blue lotus

white lotus

The lotus, or water lily, is a very important symbol in Egypt. The Egyptian blue lotus opens in the morning and sinks underwater in the evening. The Egyptian white lotus flowers at night and closes in the morning.

Many kinds of plants and animals live in the four regions of Egypt. Most of the animals are found by the Nile River. Many others live along the **coastline**, in the mountains, and in the deserts. These places are their habitats, where they find food.

papyrus plant

Paper from papyrus

Papyrus is a plant that grows in the **marshes** by the Nile River. A marsh is land that is covered by shallow water. A papyrus plant can grow up to ten feet (3 meters) tall. It is light and strong. Ancient Egyptians made beds, chairs, shoes, and boats from it. They used rolls of papyrus, like this one, for writing and drawing. The word "paper" comes from the word papyrus.

The hippopotamus, or hippo, is the third-biggest land animal. Hippopotamuses live by lakes or rivers in groups called **bloats**. They stay in the water during the day to keep their skin wet and cool. Staying in water also prevents hippos from getting sunburned. Hippos have short legs, but they can run faster than people can.

Scarab beetles, also known as dung beetles, were sacred animals in Ancient Egypt. A scarab pushing a ball of **dung**, or waste, reminded Egyptians of the sun god rolling the sun into the sky.

Egyptians ride camels in towns and deserts. Camels have a large hump of fatty tissue on their backs, which provides them with energy. Camels can go without water for long periods of time.

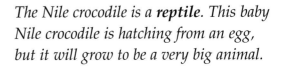

The Nile crocodile is a **reptile**. This baby Nile crocodile is hatching from an egg, but it will grow to be a very big animal.

What are pyramids?

Five thousand years ago, powerful leaders called **Pharaohs** ruled Egypt. Pharaohs were men and women who were respected by the people. They built huge **pyramids**. More than 100 of these pyramids can still be seen in Egypt today.

Pyramids are huge structures where the Pharaohs were buried after they died. The pyramids of Giza are the most famous. The statue beside them is called the Great Sphinx. It has the body of a lion and the head of a human. Egyptians believed it watched over their Pharaohs. The Sphinx is the oldest and largest statue carved from one giant stone.

Inside the pyramids

Egyptians believed that the **afterlife** was where people went after they died. The Pharaohs were buried in the pyramids with many treasures and slaves to serve them in the afterlife. Inside the pyramids were rooms and beautiful decorations. The bodies of the Pharaohs were **mummified**, or preserved. The mummy was placed inside a coffin called a **sarcophagus**, like the one on the right.

mummy

sarcophagus

King Tut

Tutankhamen (King Tut) was just nine years old when he became Pharaoh. He died when he was nineteen. Inside his tomb, people found this mask made of solid gold, as well as many treasures, such as statues, furniture, and jewelry. King Tut's treasures were brought to Toronto and New York City in 2010 so people in North America could see them.

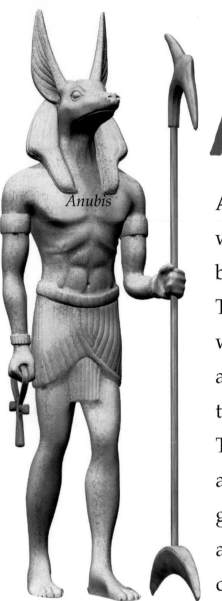
Anubis

Ancient beliefs

Ancient Egyptians, or Egyptians who lived thousands of years ago, believed in many gods and goddesses. They believed that their Pharaohs were gods, too. They built temples and **shrines**, or holy places, to show their love and respect for their gods. The old statues show Egyptian gods as half animal, half human. The sun god Ra is often shown as a man with a falcon's head. Anubis, god of the dead, had the head of a jackal.

Bastet

Eye of Horus

The Eye of Horus was a **symbol**, or sign, of protection.
It looks like the eye of a falcon with a teardrop underneath.

Cats were sacred in Egypt because they reminded people of the goddess Bastet, who had the head of a cat.

This gold and green scarab-shaped **amulet**, or charm, was believed to keep bad things away.

scarab

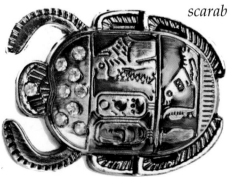

Pictures tell stories

Ancient Egyptian **myths** often talked about the lives of the gods and Pharaohs. Myths are stories that try to explain why things happen in the world around us. The myths were drawn on papyrus and told in **hieroglyphs** instead of letters. Hieroglyphs are picture words.

The myth above is about Queen Nefertari bringing gifts to the goddess Isis. The hieroglyphs are at the sides and top of the picture. What story do you think they are telling? Try making a hieroglyph story. You can draw your own pictures. Challenge your friends to guess what your story is about.

Religion today

Religion is very important to Egyptians today, as it was in the past. The main religion in Egypt is Islam. The people who follow Islam are called Muslims. Muslims read the Qur'an, the holy book of Islam, and follow the teachings of Prophet Muhammad. They pray five times a day to Allah. Allah is the Arabic name for God. About one-tenth of Egyptians are Coptic Christians. Their beliefs are based on the teachings of Saint Mark, who brought Christianity to Egypt.

minaret

(above) **Mosques** are Muslim places of worship. This is the Muhammad Ali Mosque in Cairo. A man called a **muezzin** stands on a **minaret**, or tall, thin tower and calls people to prayer.

(left) Built in 1848, the Muhammad Ali, or Alabaster, Mosque is the most famous mosque in Cairo. These Egyptian schoolchildren are visiting the mosque with their teacher.

Muslims believe that Allah spoke to Prophet Muhammad through an angel called Gabriel. Muhammad memorized Allah's words, which were then recorded in the Qur'an. The Qur'an is often placed on a stand.

Many Muslim girls and women cover their heads, especially when they read the Qur'an.

This picture shows Mary, Joseph, and baby Jesus arriving in Egypt. Christians believe Jesus is the son of God.

Coptic churches have crosses to show they are Christian churches. A community of **monks**, or religious men, lived in this old Coptic **monastery**.

23

The history of Egypt

People have lived in Egypt for thousands of years. For more than 3,000 years, Pharaohs ruled Egypt. After the Pharaohs, people from other countries ruled Egypt for most of the next 3,000 years. The rulers came from Libya, Greece, Rome, Arabia, Turkey, France, and England. The Arabs and the Turks occupied the country for many years. Egypt finally declared its **independence** in 1922, but it was still under British control until 1952.

This painting shows The Battle of the Nile in 1798, when the French fought the British for control of Egypt. The French lost the battle, and Egypt remained under British rule for another 154 years.

Egypt today

Egypt is a **republic**, a country in which people **elect** their own leaders. Egypt's main **government** is located in Cairo. A government is a group of people who lead a country. The head of the Egyptian government is the president. He and other members of the government work in a large building in Cairo called the Mugamma.

*The flag of Egypt is red, white, and black. It has an eagle **emblem** in the center. Emblems are important images. The golden eagle reminds Egyptians of Saladin, the first **sultan** of Egypt. A sultan is a strong Muslim leader who rules over many lands or people.*

Saladin wanted to build a wall that would surround both Cairo and Fustat, Egypt's first capital. The wall would keep enemies out.

*Egypt is full of buildings, such as the Saladin **Citadel**, which show its long history. A citadel is a fort that protects a city.*

Egypt's culture

oud

Egyptian **culture** is a mixture of modern ways and old traditions. Culture is the beliefs, customs, and ways of life that are shared by a group of people. It includes stories, sports, dance, music, clothing, and food.

*The goblet drum and **oud** are traditional Egyptian instruments. The oud is like a guitar.*

goblet drum

Egyptians love soccer. Their national team won the 2010 African Nations Cup. The team's nickname is "The Pharaohs."

A crafts school in Harraniya teaches children from the countryside how to use **looms**. Looms are machines for weaving cloth from **yarn**, or thread. The children design and make beautiful **tapestries**, or wall hangings with pictures woven into them. They spin their own yarn and use natural dyes made from vegetables to color it. Visitors from all over the world come here to buy their tapestries.

The tastes of Egypt

Kebabs are some of the favorite dishes of Egyptians. They are made with roasted meats and different kinds of vegetables.

Food is the delicious part of a country's culture, and the food of Egypt is very tasty! Many Egyptian dishes have come from Turkey because Egyptians lived under Turkish rule for 300 years. Egyptians use handmade **pita** bread to scoop up dips or fill them with meat, fish, or vegetables. Egyptians love spices. They like to eat pita bread with olive oil and spices.

Many kinds of spices can be found at Egyptian markets.

This boy is selling pita bread in the city. The breads are used to make pita sandwiches or are dipped into olive oil.

Turkish delights are made of chopped dates, pistachios, and hazelnuts or walnuts. They are a special treat.

Dates are a favorite food in Egypt, as well as in all Middle Eastern countries. This boy and his father are enjoying some pita bread and dates on a Muslim holiday.

Falafel is a favorite Egyptian meal. Falafels are beans that are mashed, rolled into balls, and then fried. They are served with vegetables, eaten in pita bread, or dipped into different sauces.

29

Pictures from Egypt

Each year, tourists from around the world visit Egypt. If you were a tourist, what would you like to see? What pictures would you send to your friends? Would you send pictures of the pyramids? Would you send a picture of yourself riding a camel?

Would you send a picture of yourself standing on the huge blocks at the bottom of the pyramids?

Would you send a papyrus picture with a story told in hieroglyphs?

Would you send a picture of some new friends you met in Egypt?

Would you send a picture of yourself dressed as a Pharaoh?

31

Glossary

Note: Some boldfaced words are defined where they appear in the book.

bloat A group of hippopotamuses

caravan A group of people who travel across a desert on camels

coastline The area where an ocean or sea meets land

coral reef An area of the ocean made up of living coral and skeletons of dead coral

crops Plants that are grown for food

desert A dry area with few plants and extremely hot or cold temperatures

dunes Large piles of sand created by the wind

elect To pick a leader

fertile Describing land that produces abundant crops

habitat The natural place where a plant or animal lives

hieroglyph A picture or symbol that stands for a word

independence A state of being self-governed

irrigate To bring water to dry land

kebab Pieces of meat grilled on a skewer

marsh A wetland area that is covered by water year round

mirage An image that is not really there

nomads People who move from place to place because of weather or to find food

pita A flat bread, often with a pocket

population The total number of people living in a certain place

private school A school that is not run by the government and charges fees

reptile An animal that lays eggs and has scales all over its body

tapestry A woven cloth with a design

yarn Thread used for weaving or knitting

Index